This Is A Crazy Business

The Guide To Catalytic Converter Buying

Jordan Washington

ACKNOWLEDGEMENT

I want to thank GOD for everything this industry has brought to me, and my family. Brent Evans CEO of Pro Cores for giving me the opportunity to learn and grow in this business. Shirley Washington, my grandmother may her soul Rest In Peace. She gave me the confidence to stick true to my dreams of entrepreneurship.

FOREWARD

King Jordan, I manifest you enjoying life on your terms and you will motivate others, Men and women to hustle, and most importantly, be themselves unapologetically. You, My brother UFC combat, skilled with nun-chucks and swords (seriously). Has a stripper pole in the house, dresses impeccably and sells converters out of his old school caddy. Even more because you are a young guy. Intelligent, obviously if you're doing all these cool random things. My bad, he's also a day trader. You always support me and you will have my life long support. Your resume sounds like a cheat sheet from a few players but really that's you only the boss. Cheers to all your success in future random boss activities. King Jordan is a definition of a hustler. Watch him move and read his actions. Get Motivated! Get converted, to get money!!!

I'm going to bring back some memories to King Jordan. Do you remember the first time we met? I do. I was sitting in the parking lot, I was on IG live and you were with your cousin. I opened up to go live with anyone and you came up. We had a psychological conversation about stripping and mindset game. So basically, we had our first conversation live. I remember thinking to myself who is this guy who knows all this stuff, all these swag, and sauce with the Mortal Kombat Raiden hat on LOL. Two years later I can call you a brother. You always support me, and you have my support as well. I'm proud of you because of who you are and being a coach and influencer myself, I see what you can bring and motivate others to do. Love you bro!

Enjoy your moment as this book will give you the confidence of a hustler and a certified author to accomplish all of your goals in life. See you at the top brother and if I get there first I'm ma pull you up with me. Salute to a young king, future Mogul and boss. Converter money is a mindset. It's energy. This book is a manual... for the Hustle.

Afi Kingdom

TABLE OF CONTENT

CHAPTER 1

Know The Business

(Why)

Welcome to the catalytic converter industry. Whether this is your first time or you're a seasoned veteran in this business, I'm happy to have you here. As the writer of this informative book, I want to be totally clear when I tell you this is a billion-dollar industry believe it or not. Currently, as I write this book we are at a historical all time high and the prices are through the roof but it wasn't always like this. The catalytic converter market has been non stop changing for years now through the increase of knowledge and pricing. From a system of grade categories to now over seventeen thousand individual price codes.

How: I was introduced to this greatly unique business by my friend turned mentor that started his own recycling company about ten years ago. The funny thing is when I first heard about it, I thought he was recycling canned goods but I was highly wrong. From there I was trained by one of his colleagues who showed me the ins and outs on how to navigate through this competitive industry. It's a whole new world but lucky with my previous sales experience I was able to soak up the knowledge and hit the ground running making this business my own.

My Perspective: Yes, every business is based on the obvious principles of supply and demand. But through the eyes of the viewer things can be quite different. The way I saw this business was more like the demand for an endless supply. Just think about supply and demand when the amount of a commodity, product, or service available and the desire of buyers for it, considered as factors regulating its price. In the converter industry the price of product is already regulated not by the desire of the buyers for it, but by the market on the commodity or shall I say commodities because catalytic converters contain platinum, palladium, and rhodium.

CHAPTER 2

<u>Building Clientele</u>

I n this business there are two very important words to remember and those are clientele and profit. You need both of these if you're going to continue to buy from the public. For the moment though, let's focus on clientele. What is clientele? Clientele is the collection of customers that do business with you. They are the people your company serves regularly. Think of them as the reason you do this business. It's not all about money, it's to cater to and assist the ones that have enough faith in you to trust that you'll provide them with excellent customer service and respect.

There are a few ways you can build your clientele. Like business strategies from books on entrepreneurship, but today I'll

4

explain how I have built an active and thriving clientele.

First things first, I can't stress enough how important respect is in this business. Don't insult someone's intellect, just pay them well and help them understand the business.

Number one: Befriend your customer.

See, they say business is never personal, but that doesn't mean you can't have a friendly attitude towards getting to know the person or persons you're creating a profitable transaction with. There's no harm in taking a general interest in the person you're about to pay all this money to. Get to asking them some personal information, maybe see if they have a family to take care of or hobbies they do when they aren't getting paid by you. It's always great to win a friend than pay a friend. Trust me, they'll love you for it.

The second thing you want to do to build clientele is turn your customer into a client. A customer is someone you just do business with. You know the vibes of someone who buys goods and services with you strictly transactional based, but someone who is a client is much more. A client is someone who looks to you for support and service. They have a higher level of understanding that you've established with treating them right. Simply educating them on the business will suffice as a start to turning a customer into a client.

CHAPTER 3

Dealing With Competition

Your perspective can be a double-edged sword when it comes to most topics on business nowadays. Especially when you take a look at the word competition. What is competition, whose competition, are you in competition, am I in competition? Competition is all around and within us at the same time. What is competition though? Simply put, it's the opposition you face while trying to get a task done.

Now that we know all about competition let's go down to being a good competitor. You have to compete if you want to succeed over the opposition no matter what that is. There are plenty of ways to do that but for time purposes I'll just lay out a few.

The Scorch Earth Theory: This is where you totally exhaust your area of all potential materials.

Out of town specialist: This is where you're on the road majority of the time in rural areas that don't have high paying buyers.

The shipping expert: This is where you dominate through the mail with volume.

All of these strategies have their own pros and cons but once you effectively acquire them all you'll be a force that'll put you at the top of the industry.

CHAPTER 4

<u>Staying On Top</u>

Now that we've set a clear direction on the industry, and you've built the knowledge and confidence to be a contender, let's talk about staying on top of the industry. In order to stay on top, you have to continue to be a relevant source for the public to use. You can write the best book in the world, but if nobody knows how to read, then all of that knowledge helps no one. On the other hand, if everyone gets the opportunity to glance through those amazing pages, you've helped so many people gain a wealth of knowledge which is great, because we all have heard the saying "you get paid for what you know".

CHAPTER 5

<u>Planning Success</u>

N ow that you've made the decision that you want to be a catalytic converter buyer, it's time to set a course. No successful journey gets completed without detailed navigation. On this road to cart buying, it's only natural that you might experience some bumps in the road and that's fine as long as you're prepared for them. First thing you want to have is a decent vehicle, and not just anything to get you from point A to B, but something that can haul weight. See, catalytic converters can be quite heavy by themselves. So with getting volume expect to be putting some intense strain on any vehicle. You want transportation that is built to handle heavy loads. Second thing is capital and I mean a lot of it. In today's market, it takes a small fortune to keep up with the rising cost of converters especially, when it comes to buying from knowledgeable customers that have people from all areas knocking at their doors to buy the material. Also, take in account that you want to be cash ready to make the exchange easier for the customer. To do this ties in with our third point which is having a relationship with a reliable bank. It's not everyday that people have over 6 figures let alone be trying to withdraw it. So, you want to have a clear understanding with your bank about what you do so the process with having access to cash can be as smooth as possible. Trust me, I've broken the bank literally a few times trying to satisfy my clients on a weekly basis. Once all of those aspects are taken care of, you want to develop a route. This is a small world but it's impossible to measure especially if you're not keeping track of the areas you hit. Know the places you've been to, and when you've been there, and it'll be easy to find out where you want to go in the future. And lastly, liquidating your material back to cash. You've been doing the work following the process, and now it's time you get paid. You want to do business with a trusted and reliable processor so you can continue to do your job. Let's discuss this in the next chapter.

CHAPTER 6

Call To Action

My name is Jordan Washington, and I want to personally welcome you into this unique and profitable world of catalytic converters. You've made it to the end of the book, and I hope you've learned a lot. And for the seasoned individuals, I hope this serves as a great review to you. Now I want you to put your knowledge to the test, work hard and make a bunch of money. Here at ProCores, we want to offer you and your services a home that you can trust. We will process all of your material and pay you in cash so you can quickly get back to your customers. Also, we have the largest and most informative research and development teams to keep you up to speed on today's current markets.

Don't hesitate to call or text: 804-441-3460 for all of your catalytic converter needs. We are here to help so enjoy, stay profitable, and we'll see you soon. Thank you for reading.

EXTRA CREDIT

Catalyst Company is a new business for future and striving entrepreneurs. Check out the website @ www.catalystcompanyrva.com

We've also provided an album for your listening pleasure.

Catalytic Converter Buying

Catalytic Converter Buying

Catalytic Converter Buying

Catalytic Converter Buying

_____

_____

_____

_____

_____

_____

_____

_____

_____

_____

_____

_____

_____

_____

_____

_____

_____

_____

_____

Catalytic Converter Buying

_____

_____

_____

_____

_____

_____

_____

_____

_____

_____

_____

_____

_____

_____

_____

_____

_____

_____

_____

Made in the USA
Middletown, DE
03 October 2022

11767594R00015